Before it's too late

First published 2020 by The Hedgehog Poetry Press

Published in the UK by
The Hedgehog Poetry Press
5 Coppack House
Churchill Avenue
Clevedon
BS21 6QW

www.hedgehogpress.co.uk

ISBN: 978-1-913499-02-0

Copyright © Sarah Thomson 2020

The right of Sarah Thomson to be identified as the author of this work has been asserted in accordance with the Copyright, Designs and Patents Act 1988.

All rights reserved. No part of this publication may be reproduced, stored in or introduced into a retrieval system, or transmitted in any form, or by any means (electronic, mechanical, photocopying, recording or otherwise) without prior written permissions of the publisher. Any person who does any unauthorised act in relation to this publication may be liable for criminal prosecution and civil claims for damages,

9 8 7 6 5 4 3 2 1

A CIP Catalogue record for this book is available from the British Library.

Before it's too late

by

Sarah Thomson

Contents

At the cinema 7

Lament of a Sperm Whale 8

Villanelle from Proxima b 9

In search of England 10

Silent Night 11

Brown bird 12

Poem for Katy 13

Poem for May 14

I laid bare my heart 15

White Stones 16

Christopher's Pantoum 17

The message 18

Pantoum for Sheila 19

The polyester bag 20

The Straits Hotel 21

The Rooftop Pool 22

Dahlia days 23

Incomplete 24

Wedding Triolet 25

Song for Ellen 26

AT THE CINEMA

Two shadows indistinct in the sun's blaze
As if in a cinema side by side on the beach
They sit in camping chairs content to gaze
Two shadows indistinct in the sun's blaze
The ebb and flow of tides counting their days
From each advancing wave just out of reach
Two shadows indistinct in the sun's blaze
As if in a cinema side by side on the beach

LAMENT OF A SPERM WHALE

In the toxic plastic sea
I dream as I drift bereft
there flows no breath as I hang over peaks
sheer falling away into echoing troughs
ink dark in the caverns the light is lost
skin stings salt thins temperature drops
a sudden assault three thousand feet
sharp pain no relief suckers and teeth
grief from the moment you were born still
still keeping you next to me in the toxic plastic sea
still keeping you next to me in the toxic plastic sea
grief from the moment you were born still
sharp pain no relief suckers and teeth
a sudden assault three thousand feet
skin stings salt thins temperature drops
ink dark in the caverns the light is lost

    sheer falling away   into echoing troughs
    there flows no breath   as I hang over peaks
I dream as I drift bereft   in the toxic plastic sea

VILLANELLE FROM PROXIMA B

We found your planet long ago
Our tiny spacecraft in your skies
We didn't want to let you know

Across the universe we flow
Passing by we heard your sighs
We found your planet long ago

Your sun is young and even though
In sepia light our planet dies
We didn't want to let you know

You don't notice us apropos
We think to our diminutive size
We found your planet long ago

Your earth is beautiful even so
We've looked into your elephants' eyes
We didn't want to let you know

So further onwards we will go
Your flaws are fatal we surmise
We found your planet long ago
We didn't want to let you know

IN SEARCH OF ENGLAND

He wants England back, that's what he voted for
he says the word, his face suffused with awe

he's built like a bulldog, he would be brave in war
but finding the enemy was so much easier before

still he stands resolute behind his bric-a-brac stall
dreaming of England while the pound is in freefall

his mate sells hand-grenades from his pitch next-door
imported from Holland, says after they'll cost him more

come lunchtime, they'll bond over the football score
agree next World Cup, we'll oust those Normans for sure

SILENT NIGHT

The Christmas Truce, Trêve de Noël, Weihnachtsfrieden
Bitter cold, white frost across the wires, upon the shattered shell ploughed ground
Nikolaus Sprink sings a rousing song, raises a Christmas tree
The sound of pipes, Sir Edward Hulse plans to retaliate with harmony

Bodies clad in tattered uniforms venture into no-mans-land, hand meets hand
Cigarettes exchanged for bread, buttons swapped, wine corks popped
The camera captures images, smiles as frozen faces thaw
The dead are buried, at the wake football. Voices murmur 'why do we fight this war?'

Silence at last upon the night the angel sang, the sentries stilled
A brief respite, let the mind rest where it will, drift until asleep.
The end is shocking, comes with a hiss-whine-crack and final ghastly sink
Into the mud and endless black. Back home, doorbells ring gate latches clink

In this war wilderness birds have long dropped from the sky, insects stopped
Yet one day weeds will grow, farmers return to plant their crops, harvest bones
And boots with socks, letters of love preserved in a box. The 'war to end all war'
Sixteen million fall. Next time, only shoot skywards or don't shoot at all.

BROWN BIRD

She's like
a little brown bird
neat and small
hug gently
don't squeeze
you'll break
those fragile bones

Now she's flown
I miss her
it can't be helped
any more than
the blackness
that seized me
all those years ago

Hungry cries
echo in my ears
even before
the train arrives
she misses me
once more the child
watching me walk away

Autumn dusk
and the radio
speaks of rescue
the soft accent
curling like smoke
as the trees darken
against the sky

This precious one
pecked up my trail
of crumbs
then saved me
with forgiveness
astounds me daily
with her selfless love

POEM FOR KATY

These houses that we love and leave behind
Spaces
Where the sun falls on the floor
In a particular way
As the wind in the gutter
Hums
The dust of our years settles in places too tiny for the eye to see
Atoms jostling and jogging as new feet pass by
That window where the rain still rattles a requiem from the South-West
While my homesick heart pauses to listen
For a whisper
In a whisker we are gone but the houses endure
The broken bread bin flaps in the porch
The lino in the hall bubbles
Blue dragonflies swarm on the nursery walls
Momentarily
Be kind - rip up my carpets, strip off my wallpaper, wrench up my
floorboards
For your complicated plumbing
But leave my grand front door with the important pillars and the brass
door knocker
For another century or so
Green flamed leaves on the fireplace tiles still grow
Let it be
That we can let them go
These houses that we love and leave behind

POEM FOR MAY

What can I say, May, in my poem for you?
Sometimes I see you reclining on a swing seat
Under a scalloped canopy.
Today I found you in a deckchair,
Your warm smiling face with an oversized sunflower
Drooping over you like a rain shower
So many drops of love falling.
Did you hear my mother calling?
I have some letters too – one which says:
'I think May is a bit better today'
And sure enough, there you are on a tennis court, leaning against the net
With Bill (later they'll send him their deepest regret).
White suit and hat, blue spotted blouse
With matching button shoes.
Although - how would I know?
The photographs are cream and brown.
On the back of one in faded ink:
'Sweetheart, it was a perfect honeymoon'
Gone too soon; you were gone too soon I think.

I LAID BARE MY HEART

I laid bare my heart to a linear accelerator
and it took it's time as it eyed me up
and it clicked and whirred
in that room lined with lead
all humankind fled
save me on a bed
of steel
I trembled, arms over my head
and the false blooms of spring
on the ceiling blushed pink
like my skin
as I cooked from within

WHITE STONES

Excerpt from Weymouth New Testament
'Let all who have ears give heed to what the Spirit is saying to the Churches. He who overcomes--to him I will give some of the hidden Manna, and a white stone; and--written upon the stone and known only to him who receives it-- a new name.' Revelation 2:17

There's a place not far
An oasis from the strange
With space to dream and wait for Manna
By the Kasbah gate. Those with an ear will hear
Spirits walk in the garden of this white rock place.
Will wait for a stone with a new name known
Only to those who overcome; don't roam
Too far from this space
This white rock Home.

CHRISTOPHER'S PANTOUM

(written on the day Christopher flies from Savannah, Georgia to Bellingham, Washington State)

Christopher take to the sky Christopher fly
The beat of the Monarch wing mile after mile
Four generations and back to the same tree
Warm south cold North his fluttering heart fragile

The beat of the Monarch wing mile after mile
A milkweed metamorphosis spinning silk
Warm south cold North his fluttering heart fragile
From old body parts a luminous chrysalis

A milkweed metamorphosis spinning silk
Warm west cold east the generations roam
From old body parts a luminous chrysalis
Magic moments just for a week or so

Warm west cold east the generations roam
How does a butterfly know which way to go?
Magic moments just for a week or so
Memories of more than a hundred years

How does a butterfly know which way to go?
I sit here drinking tea thinking of this
Memories of more than a hundred years
Christopher take to the sky Christopher fly

THE MESSAGE

I'm sorry not to have been back in touch with you, but things have been a little trying, I hope to correct that in due course, Les

Even though the times are trying now
And life is slipping quietly from his clutch
He intends to write a letter soon somehow
Even though the times are trying now
And lying in his bed with fevered brow
He worries that he hasn't been in touch
Even though the times are trying now
And life is slipping quietly from his clutch

PANTOUM FOR SHEILA

And now your name is written on the stone
Relentless Chronos dropping pebbles to earth
Sending the wind to shiver the creaking yews
And the grey horse watching, watching from the hill

Relentless Chronos dropping pebbles to earth
We make our way at noon from church to well
And the grey horse watching, watching from the hill
Wishing the space, the space on the stone still blank

We make our way at noon from church to well
Coins falling through dark water, dropping down
Wishing the space, the space on the stone still blank
Fossils fresh faced and softly scrubbed wink back

Coins falling through dark water, dropping down
You are more than chrono-photography to me
Fossils fresh faced and softly scrubbed wink back
Wind rustles the ivy, the pergola creaks

You are more than chrono-photography to me
I see a pair of scissors just like yours
Wind rustles the ivy, the pergola creaks
I put my fingers just where yours once went

I see a pair of scissors just like yours
The leaded lights are glowing in the dark
I put my fingers just where yours once went
Your wedding ring is on my finger now

The leaded lights are glowing in the dark
The gates are closed to guests, the cake all gone
Your wedding ring is on my finger now
And now your name is written on the stone

THE POLYESTER BAG

The
beige
bag that
was yours is
now with me and how
I wish that you could know I take
it everywhere I go, you would be so surprised!

THE STRAITS HOTEL

        The
        Straits
        Hotel
    you checked out
    fifty years ago
  I was too late Jahor Bahru
things we do when those we've loved live only in the past

THE ROOFTOP POOL

I
swim
at night
Singapore
rooftops all around
and the water turns to frosted
glass as I drift sideways under the whispering palms

DAHLIA DAYS

Doug grew Dahlias for Rose
Single-flowered, Collarette
And soon their garden overflows

Surplus tubers for us all
Wrapped in paper – keep them dry!
Semi-cactus, pompon, ball

Orange, salmon, clashing pink
Klankstad Kerkrade, Polar Sight
I left them in the kitchen sink

Garish, vulgar – not for me
A 50s nightmare, let them rot
A flower for the elderly

And driving now through Somerset
A cottage garden has them still
And only now do I regret

The Autumn Fire and Ruwenzori
That happy hotchpotch mixed up mash
Blooming gone in all their glory

So I plant Dahlias, watch them grow
Dedham soon so Can-Can now
And let my garden overflow

INCOMPLETE

Hopeful that one day we'd meet
I wondered were you near or far
Without you I was incomplete

Would you see me and retreat?
If I were waiting in a bar
Hopeful that one day we'd meet

Would I miss you on the street?
Or drive right past you in a car
Without you I was incomplete

I listened out for your heart beat
Searched for it with my radar
Hopeful that one day we'd meet

Now I've found it life is sweet
Where I am, there you are
Without you I was incomplete

I know I've fallen on my feet
And wished upon a lucky star
Hopeful that one day we'd meet
Without you I was incomplete

WEDDING TRIOLET

There's beauty in reality, I'll see you down the years
We'll dance into the future, choose the steps that rhyme
I love your equanimity, you listen to my fears
There's beauty in reality, I'll see you down the years
Finding sweetness in the bitter, laughter in the tears
Our meeting was a miracle, together in space and time
There's beauty in reality, I'll see you down the years
We'll dance into the future, choose the steps that rhyme

SONG FOR ELLEN

Born with no memory
Of life before
Made out of dust from stars
Worlds to explore
Learning conquering fears
But time it runs away from us
Over the years

If we are lucky
One day we're grown
Thinking we know it all
We leave our home
Hoping the right path appears
But time it runs away from us
Over the years

Willingly, we cast off each chain
Yet anchored together we remain

Our ships sail through storms
To far-away lands
We flounder upon the rocks
Cross shifting sands
Waiting 'til the mist clears
But time it runs away from us
Over the years

If we are fortunate
We stay in the game
Each day brings challenges
No two are the same
Seeking the music of spheres
But time it runs away from us
Over the years

Loved ones leave, we know little more
Our memories, piled like pebbles on the shore

What can I tell you?
Before you have flown
And had the chance to make
Mistakes of your own
Live life with love my dear
And time it runs away from us
Over the years

Over the years

Hear Sarah and Ted Egar perform Song For Ellen *on YouTube*

www.ingramcontent.com/pod-product-compliance
Lightning Source LLC
Chambersburg PA
CBHW021455080526
44588CB00009B/862